Through Their Eyes!

Poems of the Unseen

Debjani Bardhan Roy

BookLeaf Publishing
India | USA | UK

Made with ❤ on the BookLeaf Publishing Platform
www.bookleafpub.in
www.bookleafpub.com

Dedication

To younger Me, I am so proud you did this.
To older Me, You'll be glad you did this.

Preface

Alright, buckle up buttercup! Forget the hushed tones for a sec. You're about to dive headfirst into the secret shenanigans that go down in a girl's room when the human's not looking. Think Toy Story, but with way more angst and maybe a touch of glitter. We're talking the battle-scarred teddy bear who's seen things, the sassy stack of novels dishing literary shade, the mirror with opinions on everything, and even that pile of laundry plotting its escape. Seriously, this room? It's a regular soap opera, except the actors are, well, us.Ever wonder what your stuff really thinks? Like, does that chipped mug secretly judge your coffee choices? Does that poster roll its eyes every time she plays the same song on repeat? Does the bed judge you for sleeping too much? Spoiler alert: probably. We see it all – the late-night tears, the bursts of laughter, the frantic searches for lost earrings. We soak it up like a spilled latte.So, ditch the dusty tomes for a minute and get ready for some seriously quirky poetry. We're not just decorations; we're the unsung heroes (and occasional villains) of her daily life. Get ready to hear our side of the story. It's gonna be a wild ride, promise. Welcome to the inside scoop - You are stepping into a world as seen by those who never blink..

Acknowledgements

I am thankful to everyone who chose to be by my side even when it was hard.

To my parents, sister, friends and my grandmother, who passed on the habit of reading as a genetic gift.

1. The Chair.

I wait for her as shadows grow,
In my quiet corner, dim and low.
Through restless nights and weary days,
I hold my place, yet never sway.

She stumbles in, her soul worn thin,
A tired sigh, a fragile grin.
Sometimes, she throws her world on me;
A heap of her worn down fabric.

Yet, other nights, she finds her seat,
Curling with folded feet.
Her laughter hums like the moon's light.
Her sorrows linger throughout the night.

I watch her in the mirror's glow,
Tracing stories, I will never know.
She seeks herself in glasses so tall,
Yet never sees me there at all.

Still I remain her very own steadfast throne,
Her silent guard when she's alone.
Made of wood, I couldn't give her what blood could;
Yet bound to her, as it should.

So though she never speaks my name,
I hold her just the same.
For I am hers, through thick and thin,
The silent chair, where she has been.

2. The Mirror.

I was her, each time her gaze met mine,
A quite presence, steady in time.
Yet she never held her eyes too long,
As if afraid I would prove her wrong.

She was not one to seek my grace,
No practiced smile, no perfect face.
Perhaps she feared what I could see;
A truth unspoken, wild and free.

They say I break with careless hands,
Yet no one speaks of how I stand.
Cracked or whole, I serve the same,
Holding moments, keeping names.

She looks at me, and strength is found,
Other times, her tears fall down.
Some days, she lingers, lost in thought,
Others, she turns away distraught.

New faces pass, they come and go,
yet I reflect them, let them show.
But the white wall stays, unchanged unproved;
A silent backdrop, nothing proved.

I've watched her dance to songs Unkown,
Seen joy and sorrow softly shown.
Her laughter rings, though I stay still,
I cast it back, but feel no thrill.

Mirror-mirror, often blamed,
Who decides the beauty named?
Nor I, nor words, nor passing eyes,
But the fire within that never dies.

3. The Bed.

I lie still;
as stagnant as the resting giants of nature,
rooted deep in silence,
yet humming quietly with life.
I don't have the soul to move, they say,
But I know souls like no other,
The shifting of dreams, The turning of thoughts,
the slow surrender of Burdens
as Bodies melt into me.

I am stitched with memory,
padded with whispered secrets,
soaked in the salt of tears and the sweat of love.
Oh! The Human touch!

She comes with the scent of rain and daydreams,
her hair a tangle of yesterday's thoughts,
Eyes glazed with sleep or sorrow
or stories from the fairies.
For a while. I become her world,
Her refuge, her confessional,
He escape from the noise,
Who demands her name.

I watch her rise,
scorched from heaven to concrete,
from heaven to concrete,
from warmth to war,
Pulling on her armor of denim and doubt.

The sheets cling to her,
Like I want her not to go,
She leaves anyway,
But she returns,
She always does,
So I wait,
patient as stone, soft as love,
Not just a bed,
but a silent witness,
to the beating heart of human life.

4. The Cupboard.

I stand; upright,
unmoving and as strong as a tree.
A silent sentinel in the corner,
my spine built of oak and wood and hinges,
my belly full of forgotten seasons.

They call me lifeless,
A box of utility,
But within me, Time itself,
Is just folded neatly.

No heartbeat, they say.
Yet I hold the pulse of routine,
the soft rhythm of daily rituals:
The choosing chaos
Or the Changing Intimacy,
or the Quite Indecision of morning hours.

I am quite known to her,
The one with hurried hands,
the sight that blooms like a wildflower,
Like parting the veil of memory.
Each corner a diary,
Each shelf, a shrine.

She rarely sees me.
Like a distant frame,
In the painting of her life.
But I see her,
In every flung open door,
In every outfit tossed,
From a hopeful lover,
to a hard headed professional,
She brushes past,
perhaps to hide something in me,
perhaps to seek something in me.

I don't speak to her,
I simply hold,
In fabric,
In fragrance,
In fragments.

5. The Glass of Red wine.

She reached for me with trembling grace,
Fingers curved like twilight lace.
I felt her pulse, a silent symphony,
And knew, tonight, her ache had come.

My body brimming, rich and red,
The wine within, not words but said:
'Drink deep, forget, remember slow,
I know the things you'll never show".

Her lips met mine,
Each time, with less concern for vice.
The first a question,
the second a fire,
the third an echo of desire.

Eyes filled with Red wine's
hazy spell,
Lost in the pull that she knew too well.
As the clock struck 2:42,
She sighed soft 'Be gentle,You'.

Did I drink her or did she drink me?
I watched her fall, then gently rise,

Storms swirling quite in her eyes,
And I the fragile glass,
Still wondered,
with the remaining pieces,
Of her warmth as tracer,
Was is it red wine?
Or a lover's sign?

6. The Books.

We gather dust, but not regret.
Stacked sideways, bent, a little wet,
from tea stained nights and weeping skies,
Her fingers graced the inches of our sides,
But, She used to touch us with her eyes.

Silence swells where Stories lived,
her fingers pause and her eyes stop,
And oh, we don't want her to go,
Pausing on covers worn and torn
as if to ask "was I reborn?"

We have heard the quite in her sighs,
seen the sleep stuck in her eyes.
She tiptoes near, soul half - asleep,
Falling from dreams, too hard to keep.

We have seen her eyes gleam starlight,
Her tears salt the margins of tragic ends,
Her laughter tuck into the creases
The moment her favorite protagonist eases.

She always forger her coffee on the table,
But that isn't our tale to tell,

We mock the coffee for going cold,
As if we know, It will be us,
She's forever gonna hold.

We are her loyal relics,
She might return,
smelling like the world,
But always need a Book,
To feel whole.

7. The Window.

I cradle the hush between her hours,
The in between of day's clutter,
and night's unwritten longing.
A pane of breathless distance,
I stand sentinel as she fold into herself,
Backlit by the hues,
She never names aloud.

She leans close,
forehead grazing my frame,
Not in affection, but in search.
The world beyond me,
Is a language
she has still been learning,
shadows stretching from street lamps,
The gush of lives,
She quite doesn't touch.

She opens me,
Like a gateway to her freedom,
Soft rustles of leaves,
The clinking rhythm,
Of the birds singing.

I remember her younger,
All fire and flight,
Talking to the stars,
Like they'll reply.
To the sun as a challenge,
To look into his eyes,
To the moon,
Like she will smile back.

She now, often,
Pulls the draped closed
I don't protest.
I remain the border of dreams,
A witness to her changing weather,
The carrier,
Of her undisputed fingerprints.

8. The Table.

I am where her chaos,
Learns to sit still.
Not orderly; Never that,
But familiar,
like the rhythm of her heart.
Failing every time,
She tries bringing stature.

She arrives with a storm in her arms,
Half written notes, Unpublished papers,
Teacups, half-full of resolve.
Pens scattered like fallen soldiers,
highlighters bleeding neon urgency,
The notepad, from somebody special.

She never apologizes for all her mess,
I like her that way,
It's the shape of her mind,
That I carry,
Laid bare in Ink and attention.

My surface bears,
The scars of her seasons,
A cut mark, from her laptop stand,

The faint curl of coffee stains,
Every blemish a testament,
To nights spent chasing meaning,
to her struggles,
Through Paragraphs, Proficiency and Possibility.

And though my exteriors,
Are all wood,
My insides carry secrets,
She hides.
Dreams she decides,
Deadlines that she will pass,
Life, that she writes.

9. The Coffee mug.

I am warmth, briefly held,
A small comfort cupped between hands
that often tremble from things
no one else can see.
She doesn't choose me for beauty.

My glaze is chipped,
My print half-faded,
But I am hers;
Chosen every night,
Like her favorite song,
Every morning,
Like a ritual.

I know the heat of her urgency,
The pause of her distraction,
She often forgets me,
Burning with brew,
Her hands linger to her unkempt books,
Her return,
Just a little more than late.

She hides her face behind me sometimes,
I am aligned with her beliefs,

She thinks, overall.
Bitterness, warmth
and occasionally,
The weight,
Of her unspoken miseries,
submerge into my vapor,
Of fresh brew.

10. The Fan.

I turn, tirelessly,
above the slow unravel of her days,
She rarely looks up at me,
Yet I am always watching,
Spinning circles through her stillness,
softening the sharp edges of her thoughts.

My hum is a lullaby,
for her restlessness.
I've sung her to sleep
on nights when even the stars
seemed too distant to trust.

I've murmured through monsoons,
through heatwaves,
through heartbreaks,
Each rotation, that whispers,
I'll always be here.

She stares at me dead,
On nights of her distress,
Her eyes glaze over,
tracking my circles,
I wish I could slow the world for her,

ease the tightness,
Offer more than just,
The turning of tired air.

I am here,
Above her sorrows,
above her joys,
above it all,
Circling endlessly,
Synonymous to her faith,
With no name.

11. The Door.

I creak with grace,
I groan with time,
She passes through me,
Day and night,
With heavy hearts or sprits light.
Sometimes, she pauses,
Hand on me,
As the world beyond,
Is too tame.

She doesn't knock,
She doesn't speak,
But I can hear thoughts,
that leak.
The worries trailing on her skin,
the storms she fights,
But hides within.

I've heard her laugh on my side,
and tears she thought,
She needed to hide.
Slammed in anger,
Or closed with care,
I've held her secrets in the air.

I've felt the rush of incoming friends,
The hopeful starts, the quite ends.
Strangers footsteps,
Lover's lies, hellos,
that came with fast goodbyes.
Her safe escape, her closing door,
No matter what she's running from,
I am the place she calls 'come home'.

12. The Lamp.

I rise when shadows stretch their reach,
Casting hush across the peach
Of evening walls and window frames,
Where nothing moves, But silenced flames.
I see her in cluttered grace,
A furrowed brow, a focused face.

She taps me on,
no words, No glance,
Just seeks my glow to help her dance,
through labyrinths,
Of Ink and thought,
Fighting battles,
Silence brought.

I've watched her grin,
without a sound,
A story found, a line unbound.
thoughts that refuse to bend,
The line she wrote,
Not quite the end.
I do not stray,
I hold her when she slips away.

She leaves her undone business,
scattered in clues,
But I am an expert at keeping trace,
A circle cast, a sacred space.
No medal, crown, or loud acclaim;
I cradle her in muted gleam,
the keeper of her midnight dream.

13. The Soundbox.

I wait in silence, calm and still,
Until her fingers seek the thrill,
A button pressed, and I wake,
to break the hush,
To make the hearts ache.
She never asks, but I comply,
A charade to match her sky.

I've held her blues,
Her late night Bollywood concerts,
Her Stormy beats,
Her anthems pulsing through the sheets.
She plays me loud when she's alive,
And soft when trying to survive.

Sometime she sings,
Not quite on cue,
But sweet in ways the stars would rue.
I hold her voice,
Her cracking tone,
A voice made of skin and bone.
She turns me up to down regret,
turns me down but never forgets.

And when the room grows still again,
No chords to mask the duo refrain,
I power down, but do not erase,
Her touch still fresh on my face.
For I am just sound and shell,
But where her hidden aura dwells.

14. The Carpet.

I lie in wait, beneath it all,
The hurried steps, the stumbles and falls.
A canvas for her quite tread,
The place she lands,
The place she's led.

Not grand, not praised,
But every thread of me,
Is tied to her dreams.
Her mornings start upon my weave,
Her nights also,
Are a candid affair,
Her pace in looping tracks,
Her joy, her pain, hr aching backs.

I wear the wear she doesn't name,
but still remains unchanged; The same.
The untalkative witness, ever near,
Who gathers all she drops right here,
I carry memory in my thread,
The life she walks, the words she's said.

So while the world may call me low,
I am where her quite moments grow.

She would think I am magical,
if ever I could tell her She was the magic,
Her Unnoticed carpet,
Not Just a floor, But ground and grace;
The silent center of her space.

15. The Pile of clothes.

We are in the between,
Not quite worn,
Not quite clean.
Folded once with care,
And the slumped, collapsed,
In the corner of her chair.

We carry yesterday's hours,
The scent of her skin,
Traces of laughs,
Hints of frowns,
A sleeve remembers,
How she searched for light,
The forgotten sock at the bottom,
Still hopes to see her sight.

We are her pause,
Her inexact grace,
A silent rebellion, against a perfect place.
No Ironed truth, no polished face,
Just layers of her being,
In the quite space.

She often ignores us,

A whispered 'Later' when see crosses us,
But we are proof,
That she has been here,
Not mess, But memory.
Not burden, But trace.
We are the life,
She doesn't erase.

16. The Couch.

I cradle her when the world forgets,
When she sinks like dusk, in quite sweats.
A refuge carved in chord and thread,
Where restless thoughts,
are softly spread.
She doesn't talk with her lips,
But in the way her posture slips.

A movie plays, a mug in tow,
Her joy returns in sudden flow,
I hold her happy as I hold her ache,
No Judgments passed, no heart to break.
The cushion knows her shifting moods,
The long delays between her foods.

The way she curves, all alone,
Her need for softness, flesh and bones,
I have worn her shape a thousand ways,
A portrait cast in quite days.
She sits on me with honest pace,
And yet no one fits her sacred space.

I may sag beneath the strain,
But I would hold her,

Through it all again,
For I am more than cloth and frame,
More than furniture without a name,
I am her shelter, bruised and True,
And she always returns,
As dreamers do.

17.

18. The Pillow.

I am the last,
She touches at night,
When the world fades,
And dims her light.
She presses her dreams,
With breath half-held,
And eyes weary of her past.

Her tears don't shout,
They mostly are on a silent spree,
Where their ultimate destination,
Is to land on me.
Her glowing spark, refuses confusion,
An uncanny woman,
With her bizarre manifestations.

Sometimes she clutches,
Sometimes she throws,
Her dreams are fragments,
Sometimes Ice and sometimes fire,
In tangled plots and lost desire.

I maybe small, not much to see,
But decades pass by,

As she leans on me.
Her soft companion, Ever still,
Who bends to shape her dreamy will.
I hold it all,
Each shade she feels,
I gently keep,
Her softest storms,
Her deepest sleep.

19. The Suitcase.

I sit in the shadows,
Zipped but breathing,
Half forgotten, yet never leaving.
A quietness to her gloom,
Tucked by the corner of her room.

I am not always still and bare,
There are times,
When I dance from here to there.
I have rolled through airports,
Train-bound tracks,
With stuffed aspirations and hurried packs.

I have held her nervous mess,
The chaos of a last minute dress.
Perfume sealed in scarves and thread,
Thoughtful letters, She carefully kept.
Tickets faded, Coins once bright,
Worn out laces, Tangled tight.

I wait for the time,
When she pulls me back to light,
The familiarity of home,
Or the excitement of a new stone,

I am the only one with privilege,
The privilege to see her,
Even when,
She's out of that gigantic door.

20. The Curtains.

I dance with the wind,
I hide the light,
I frame her mornings and her softer nights,
Drawn open or pulled in tight,
I watch her live in shade and bright.
I sway in rhythm to her sighs,
A veil between her and the skies.

Through me, She watches raindrops fall,
The quite ache of dusk's soft call.
She lingers here with that weird mug,
Shifting between the reality and
Her Illusion's thug.
She stares, lost in the blue,
As if the world outside withdrew.

I catch the scent of roses, Ink,
A paper's edge, a drying sink.
The outside calls in distant tunes,
But she calls herself,
The child of the Moon.
I stretch, I hover, soft, unseen,
A boundary between the still and keen.

The window loses her sight,
When I am draping her through time,
I do not plead, I do not cling,
In glances cast, in corners turned,
In laughter brief and heartbreak learned.
A mystery of subtle ease,
A melody that lingers,
A reminder,
Her mind won't cease.

21. Through their eyes!

"She flops on me like Royalty" said the chair proudly.
"She pouts at me like I am to blame,
But I never started this game" replied the mirror,
profusely.
The bed rolled it's eyes "She struggles to differ,
Between a nap and zoning out in my lap"
"She hides her yesteryears in my chest,
but never really rests" sighed the cupboard.

"She stares through me, Lost in thought,
Some battles can't really be fought' said the glass upright.
"But she's rarely there". Replied the books,
"You are just too busy to care" snapped the window,
"She taps her fingers when she's unsure"
Spoke the old wrinkly table,
"I haven't seen people who like me,
This Ice cold" said the coffee mug.

"Nevertheless her chaos always wins" The fan laughs
from above,
"It still hurts, from being slammed the night before"
Opened up a tired door,
"At least SHE doesn't have a switch,
To dim her sparkle" smirked the lamp.

"She just found a new favorite song"
Hummed the soundbox.
"Her feet are cold, But her heart? A flare",
Said the carpet, collecting her hair.
"Do you think today's the day we clean out?",
Asked the weary pile of clothes.

"She hasn't been her, lately, would take time"
Replied the Couch, The oldest of all.
"Her nights also have been in quite the slouch"
Joined the Pillow in the talk.
"Could be from her last trip of enchantment".
Said a Proud Suitcase.
"Hush! She's here" Alerted the Door.
"She hides, then peeks,
Will she ever know,
She IS the poem the Whole House speaks?"
The curtain spoke,
While they all saw her,
In the space which was hers,
In the space which was theirs.